3 6 9 Manifest

This journal belongs to:

_____

Copyright © 2023 by Belffy Books
All rights reserved. Copyright and other intellectual property laws protect these materials. Reproduction or retransmission of the materials, in whole or in part, in any manner, without the prior written consent of the copyright holder, is a violation of copyright law.

Celebrate your progress and check off each day of your efforts!

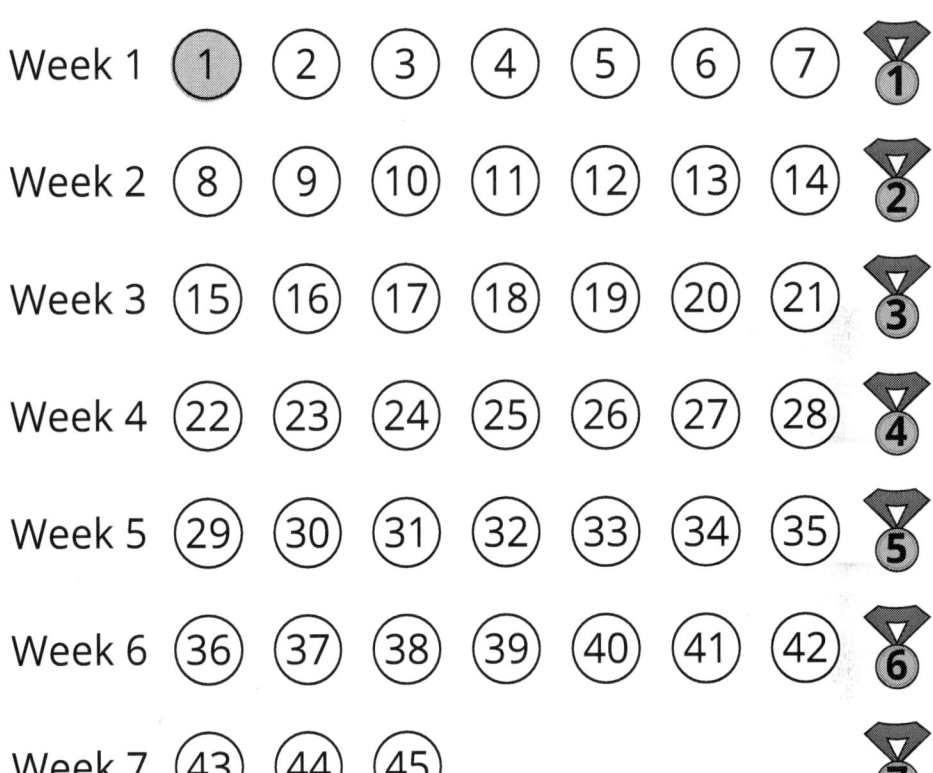

The act of writing down your manifestation every day is an important part of the manifestation process. By regularly writing down your manifestation, you are creating a daily reminder for yourself of what you are trying to manifest. This can help to keep you focused and motivated on achieving your goals. Additionally, writing down your manifestation can help to clarify your thoughts and give you a better understanding of what you are trying to manifest. This can be especially helpful if you are feeling unsure or uncertain about what you want to manifest.

Overall, being consistent with writing down your manifestation every day is an important part of the manifestation process. It can help to keep you focused, motivated, and accountable for achieving your goals.

WHAT IS 3 6 9?

The 3 6 9 method is a spiritual practice that involves using the power of your mind and significant numerical patterns to manifest your dreams and desires into reality. This method is based on the law of attraction, which states that we attract into our lives the things that we focus on, whether positive or negative. By aligning ourselves with the frequency of the numbers 3 6 9, we can tap into their power to manifest our intentions and bring our dreams to fruition.

The numerical reasoning behind this practice is based on the concept of frequency. Everything in the universe vibrates at its own unique frequency, and by aligning ourselves with certain frequencies, we can access the power of those vibrations to manifest our desires. The numbers 3 6 9 are considered to be significant in this practice because they are considered to be the most powerful and transformative numbers in the universe.

Nikola Tesla, the famous inventor, and scientist believed that the true power of the universe could be unlocked through the understanding and use of the numbers 3 6 9. He claimed that if you want to have the key to the universe, you need to know the true power of the numbers 3 6 9. Nikola tesla was known for his extraordinary inventions that we use every day and believed that if you integrate 3 6 9 into your daily routine, you can unlock ones true potential.

Introducing the 369 Manifestation Method

The 369 Manifestation Method is a powerful tool for manifesting your desires and goals. It is based on the belief that our thoughts and emotions are like seeds that we plant in our minds, and as we focus on these thoughts and feelings, they grow and manifest in our lives. This method involves using visualization, positive affirmations and gratitude to help manifest your desires. By using the 369 Manifestation Method you can take control of your life and create the reality you desire.

The first step in using the 369 Manifestation Method is to identify what it is that you want to manifest. This can be anything from a new job or career to a new relationship, to financial abundance, or even better health. Once you have identified your desire, the next step is to focus on it and visualize it in your mind.

Next, you will use positive affirmations to help reinforce your desire and bring it into your reality. These affirmations can be short, simple statements that affirm your desire and affirm that you are capable of manifesting it. For example, if you are trying to manifest a new job, you might use affirmations like "I am worthy of a fulfilling and rewarding career" or "I am capable of attracting the perfect job for me".

Finally, you will use gratitude to help manifest your desire. By focusing on what you are grateful for, you can help bring your desire into your reality. This can be as simple as writing down a list of things you are grateful for each day or expressing gratitude in your daily affirmations.

By using the 369 Manifestation Method regularly, you can begin to see positive changes in your life. You can use this method to manifest your desires and goals and create the life you want to live.

TIPS TO AMPLIFY YOUR MANIFESTATION

Take some time to sit in a comfortable position, close your eyes, and focus on your breath. As you inhale and exhale, imagine yourself in a peaceful and serene environment, surrounded by positive energy.

Once you feel calm and centered, begin to recite your affirmations. Speak them with conviction and belief, as though you are already in possession of the thing you are trying to manifest.

After each set of affirmations, take 17 seconds to visualize yourself with the thing you are trying to manifest. Imagine yourself holding it, using it, or enjoying it in some way. Tap into the emotions of having this thing and believe it is real.

Phrase your affirmations as though you have the thing you're manifesting. For example: "I am so grateful and my heart is so full that I received $10,000 this week."

THE SIGNIFICANCE OF THE NUMBERS 3 6 AND 9

The numbers 3, 6, and 9 hold great significance in the universe and consistently show up in various ways. For example, the digital root of a perfect circle is 9, as it is the result of adding up the digits 3, 6, and 0. This is not the only instance in which these numbers appear in relation to circles.

If we divide a circle into two equal halves, we are left with 180 degrees. The digital root of 180 is also 9. When we further divide one of these halves into two equal parts, we are left with 90 degrees. The digital root of 90 is also 9.

This pattern continues as we divide each half into smaller and smaller parts. For example, if we divide 90 in half, we are left with 45 degrees. The digital root of 45 is 9. If we continue dividing 45 in half, we are left with 22.5 degrees, the digital root of which is also 9. This pattern continues on and on, always resulting in the number 9.

This consistent appearance of the numbers 3, 6, and 9 in relation to circles and their divisions indicates their significance in the universe. These numbers may hold the key to understanding deeper mysteries of the universe and the fundamental principles of reality.

HOW TO USE THIS JOURNAL

Before getting started, it's important to take some time to really think about what it is you want to manifest. This will help you create a clear and focused affirmation that will be more effective in manifesting your desired outcome.

Once you're clear on your intention, it's time to create your affirmation. This should be a short and expressive sentence that states your desired manifestation in the present tense as if it's already happening. For example: "I am so happy and my heart is so full now that I have $10,000 extra in my checking account" or "I am so grateful to have been hired for my dream job!"

How to manifest your dream:

Write your desire 3 times in the morning.

Write your desire 6 times in the afternoon.

Write your desire 9 times in the evening.

As you write, focus on how it will feel when you achieve your desired outcome and imagine yourself already living it.
It's also important to repeat this process for at least 33-45 days in a row. This will help create a strong and consistent focus on your desired manifestation, increasing its likelihood of manifesting in your reality.
Once you've repeated this process for the prescribed number of days, it's important to let go and trust that your desire will manifest in its own time. This means not getting too attached to a specific outcome or timeline, and being open to the universe bringing you something even better than what you originally intended.
By following these steps and focusing on your desired manifestation consistently, you can manifest your dream and bring it into reality.

Understanding the Power of Visualization

The first thing to understand about visualization is that it is the act of creating mental images of the things we want to manifest in our lives. This can be anything from a new car to a fulfilling relationship to a successful career. The key is to be specific and detailed in our visualizations, seeing ourselves as if we already have these things in our lives.
Visualization activates the subconscious mind, which is a powerful force that shapes our reality. When we visualize our desires, we are sending a clear message to our subconscious mind that we want these things to manifest in our lives. This sets in motion a series of events that can lead to the manifestation of our desires.
To visualize your desires effectively, it is important to use all of your senses. Imagine the sights, sounds, smells, tastes, and feelings of your desired outcome. The more vivid and detailed your visualization, the more powerful it will be. Additionally, it is crucial to visualize your desires with a positive mindset and a sense of gratitude. This helps to attract positive energy and increase the likelihood of manifestation.
Finally, it is important to visualize your desires consistently. This means setting aside time each day to visualize your desires, as well as incorporating visualization into your daily routine. By making visualization a regular part of your life, you can effectively manifest your desires and create the life you desire.
In summary, a visualization is a powerful tool that activates the subconscious mind and can lead to the manifestation of our desires. By being specific and detailed, using all of our senses, and practicing visualization consistently, we can effectively use visualization to create the life we desire.

"If you knew the magnificence of 3, 6, and 9, you would have a key to the universe."

- NIKOLA TESLA

Using Positive Affirmations to Manifest Your Desires

Positive affirmations are an essential tool in the 369 Manifestation Method because they help to reprogram your subconscious mind. By repeating positive affirmations, you are replacing negative thoughts and beliefs with positive ones. This shift in thinking allows you to align with your desires and manifest them in your life.

One of the key things to remember when using positive affirmations is to focus on the present tense. This means that your affirmations should be written as if they are already happening in your life. For example, instead of saying, "I want to be rich," you would say, "I am rich." This sends a clear message to your subconscious mind that you already have what you desire and it helps to attract that reality into your life.

To make your positive affirmations even more powerful, it is important to visualize yourself experiencing your desired outcome. This means that you should take a few moments each day to close your eyes and imagine yourself living the life you desire. As you visualize, try to feel the emotions and sensations that you would feel if your desires were already a reality. This will reinforce the message you are sending to your subconscious mind and help to manifest your desires more quickly.

In conclusion, using positive affirmations is an effective way to manifest your desires using the 369 Manifestation Method. By creating specific, positive, and present tense affirmations, repeating them daily, and visualizing your desired outcome, you can shift your thinking and align with your desires to manifest them in your life.

In this journal, you will find an affirmation for each day that aligns with the principles of the 369 Manifestation Method. By repeating these affirmations daily, you can reinforce the message you are sending to your subconscious mind and increase the likelihood of your desires manifesting in your life.

Using Gratitude to Manifest Your Desires

In order to manifest your desires, it is crucial to cultivate an attitude of gratitude. This means taking the time to appreciate the things you already have in your life, rather than constantly focusing on what you don't have. When you express gratitude, you are sending a powerful message to the universe that you are thankful for what you have, and you are open to receiving even more.

One effective way to practice gratitude is to write down the things you are grateful for in a journal. This can be anything from the food on your plate, to the people in your life, to the simple pleasures of a sunny day. Reflect on why you are grateful for these things, and allow yourself to feel the gratitude in your heart.

Another way to cultivate gratitude is to make a daily gratitude list. Take a few minutes each day to write down at least three things you are grateful for. This can be anything from the big things in your life, like your health and relationships, to the little things, like a warm cup of coffee or a kind word from a friend.

As you focus on the things you are grateful for, you will start to notice more and more blessings in your life. Your mind will be more open to abundance and abundance will flow more freely into your life. By using gratitude to manifest your desires, you are setting the stage for the universe to bring you everything you desire and more.

The Importance of Action

The next step in the 369 Manifestation Method is to take action towards manifesting your desires. While visualization and gratitude are important tools for manifestation, they are not enough on their own. In order to truly manifest your desires, you must also take action towards bringing them into your reality.

To take action towards manifesting your desires, first identify the steps you need to take to make your desires a reality. This may involve setting goals, creating a plan, and taking small, consistent actions towards achieving those goals. For example, you want to manifest a new job, you may need to update your resume, apply for job openings, and prepare for interviews.

As you take action towards manifesting your desires, it is important to stay focused and committed. This means staying focused on your goals, and not letting distractions or setbacks derail your progress. It also means staying committed to taking consistent, small steps towards achieving your goals, even when it feels challenging or difficult.

By taking action towards manifesting your desires, you are showing the universe that you are serious about manifesting your desires. This sends a powerful message to the universe and helps to bring your desires into your reality more quickly and easily. By combining visualization, gratitude, and action, you can create a powerful manifestation process that will help you manifest your desires with ease and grace.

The Role of Patience and Persistence

The final step in the 369 Manifestation Method is to practice patience and persistence. Manifestation is not an instant process, and it can take time for your desires to manifest in your reality. Therefore, it is important to be patient and persistent as you work towards manifesting your desires.

To practice patience and persistence, remind yourself that manifesting your desires is a journey, not a destination. This means that you may encounter setbacks and challenges along the way, but you must stay focused and committed to your goals. It also means that you may not see immediate results, but you must have faith that your desires are manifesting, even if you cannot see them yet.

Another way to practice patience and persistence is to focus on the present moment. This means letting go of any worries or anxieties about the future, and instead focusing on the here and now. As you focus on the present moment, remind yourself that you are taking the right steps towards manifesting your desires and that the universe is working on your behalf.

By practicing patience and persistence, you are showing the universe that you are committed to manifesting your desires. This sends a powerful message to the universe and helps to bring your desires into your reality more quickly and easily. With patience and persistence, you can manifest your desires with ease and grace and create the life you desire.

Overcoming Limiting Beliefs

One of the biggest obstacles to manifesting your desires is limiting beliefs. Limiting beliefs are negative thoughts and beliefs that hold you back from achieving your goals. They may tell you that you are not good enough, that you are not worthy, r that you cannot achieve your desires.

To overcome limiting beliefs, it is important to identify and challenge these negative thoughts. This means becoming aware of the limiting beliefs that are holding you back and then questioning and refuting these beliefs. For example, if you have a limiting belief that you are not good enough, you can challenge this belief by reminding yourself of your accomplishments and strengths.

Another way to overcome limiting beliefs is to replace them with positive affirmations. Positive affirmations are powerful statements that affirm your worth, your power, and your ability to manifest your desires. For example, you can affirm that you are worthy, that you are deserving, and that you are capable of manifesting your desires.

By overcoming limiting beliefs, you are clearing the way for your desires to manifest. This means that you are creating space for abundance, joy, and riches to flow into your life. With practice, you can learn to overcome limiting beliefs and manifest your desires with ease and grace.

The Role of Support and Community

Another important aspect of the 369 Manifestation Method is the role of support and community. Manifestation can be a challenging process, and it can be helpful to have the support and encouragement of others. This is why it is important to surround yourself with supportive and positive people who can help you on your journey.

To find support and community, consider joining a manifestation group or workshop. These groups and workshops can provide you with a safe and supportive space to share your goals and desires, and to receive encouragement and guidance from others. You can also connect with other like-minded individuals who are on their own manifestation journey, and who can provide you with support and inspiration.

Another way to find support and community is to seek out mentors and coaches who can help you on your journey. These mentors and coaches can provide you with guidance and support and can help you overcome any challenges or obstacles that may arise. They can also help you stay focused and committed to manifesting your desires, and can provide you with valuable tools and techniques to help you manifest with ease and grace.

By surrounding yourself with supportive and positive people, you are creating a powerful network of support and encouragement. This can help you stay focused and committed to manifesting your desires, and can help you manifest your desires with ease and grace.

The Role of Faith and Trust

The final aspect of the 369 Manifestation Method is the role of faith and trust. In order to manifest your desires, you must have faith that the universe will bring you what you desire, and that you are worthy and deserving of your desires. This faith and trust are essential to the manifestation process and can help you manifest your desires with ease and grace.

To cultivate faith and trust, it is important to let go of any doubts or fears that may be holding you back. This means releasing any fears about not being good enough, not being worthy, or not being able to manifest your desires. Instead, focus on the belief that you are deserving and capable of manifesting your desires, and that the universe is working on your behalf.

Another way to cultivate faith and trust is to practice gratitude and appreciation. As you focus on the things you are grateful for in your life, you are sending a powerful message to the universe that you are thankful for what you have, and that you are open to receiving even more. This gratitude and appreciation can help you cultivate a deeper sense of faith and trust in the universe, and can help you manifest your desires with ease and grace.

By cultivating faith and trust, you are creating a powerful foundation for manifestation. This means that you are aligning yourself with the flow of abundance, and that you are creating the space for your desires to manifest in your reality. With faith and trust, you can manifest your desires with ease and grace, and create the life you desire.

MY REFLECTIONS

_____
_____
_____
_____
_____
_____
_____
_____
_____
_____
_____
_____
_____
_____
_____
_____
_____
_____
_____
_____
_____

My Top Desires:

"It's important to set your own goals and work hard to achieve them."

- YUICHIRO MIURA

DAY 1

MORNING

1. _____
2. _____
3. _____

AFTERNOON

1. _____
2. _____
3. _____
4. _____
5. _____
6. _____

What's stopping you from going after your dreams?
-------------------- --------------------

Daily Affirmations

> **I am the author of my life story.**

EVENING

> *Take the first step in faith. You don't have to see the whole staircase. Just take the first step.*

DAY 2

MORNING

1. _____
2. _____
3. _____

AFTERNOON

1. _____
2. _____
3. _____
4. _____
5. _____
6. _____

What is one of your favorite songs from your childhood?

- -

Daily Affirmations

> ❖ **I have the freedom to create any future I want.** ❖

🌙 EVENING

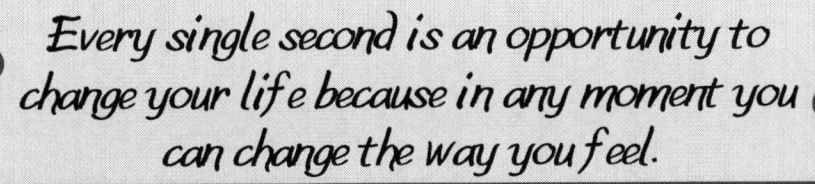

> " *Every single second is an opportunity to change your life because in any moment you can change the way you feel.* "

DAY 3

MORNING

1. _____
2. _____
3. _____

AFTERNOON

1. _____
2. _____
3. _____
4. _____
5. _____
6. _____

Who is the one friend you can always rely on?
- -

Daily Affirmations

> ❖ **Money comes to me easily and effortlessly.** ❖

🌙 EVENING

> ❝ *Believe you deserve it and the universe will serve it.* ❞

DAY 4

MORNING

1.
2.
3.

AFTERNOON

1.
2.
3.
4.
5.
6.

What is the biggest accomplishment in your personal life?
-------------------- --------------------

Daily Affirmations

> ❂ **Something wonderful is about to happen to me.** ❂

EVENING

> " *Visualize your highest self and start showing up as her.* "

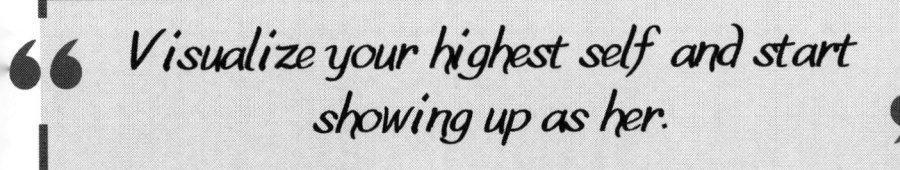

DAY 5

MORNING

1.
2.
3.

AFTERNOON

1.
2.
3.
4.
5.
6.

What is a recent purchase that has added value to your life?

Daily Affirmations

> ◆ *I have the power to create the life I desire.* ◆

EVENING

> **" Expect to manifest everything that you want to manifest. "**

DAY 6

MORNING

1.
2.
3.

AFTERNOON

1.
2.
3.
4.
5.
6.

What is the biggest lesson you learned in childhood?

Daily Affirmations

> **Whatever I put my mind to, I achieve.**

EVENING

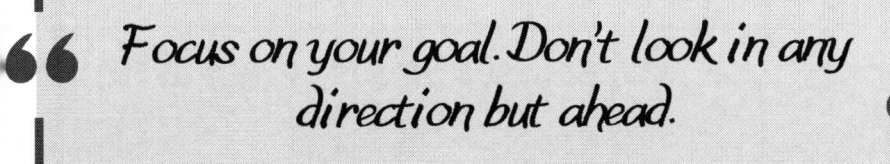

> " *Focus on your goal. Don't look in any direction but ahead.* "

DAY 7

MORNING

1. _____
2. _____
3. _____

AFTERNOON

1. _____
2. _____
3. _____
4. _____
5. _____
6. _____

How can you pamper yourself in the next 24 hours?

Daily Affirmations

I look for the good in every situation.

EVENING

> *All that we are is a result of what we have thought.*

DAY 8

MORNING

1. _____
2. _____
3. _____

AFTERNOON

1. _____
2. _____
3. _____
4. _____
5. _____
6. _____

What is your favorite part of your daily routine?

Daily Affirmations

> **I am always attracting abundance.**

EVENING

> *We receive exactly what we expect to receive.*

DAY 9

MORNING

1.
2.
3.

AFTERNOON

1.
2.
3.
4.
5.
6.

What is your favorite holiday and why do you love it?
- -

Daily Affirmations

> **I am creating the life of my dreams.**

EVENING

> "Your thoughts are the architects of your destiny."

DAY 10

MORNING

1.
2.
3.

AFTERNOON

1.
2.
3.
4.
5.
6.

What is a great book you've recently read?

Daily Affirmations

> **Great strength lies within me at all times.**

EVENING

> *Ask for what you want and be prepared to get it.*

DAY 11

MORNING

1.
2.
3.

AFTERNOON

1.
2.
3.
4.
5.
6.

What is your favorite movie and why do you love it?

Daily Affirmations

> ○ **I am aligned with the energy of abundance.** ○

EVENING

> " *A person is only limited by the thoughts that he chooses.* "

DAY 12

MORNING

1.
2.
3.

AFTERNOON

1.
2.
3.
4.
5.
6.

What is your favorite food you love to indulge in?

Daily Affirmations

> ◆ *I am worthy of manifesting my biggest desires.* ◆

EVENING

> " *Whether you think you can or can't, either way, you are right.* "

DAY 13

MORNING

1. _____
2. _____
3. _____

AFTERNOON

1. _____
2. _____
3. _____
4. _____
5. _____
6. _____

What is a major lesson that you learned from your job?
-------------------- -------------------

Daily Affirmations

> **I can do anything I put my mind to.**

🌙 EVENING

> **"** *The Universe is asking... Show me your new vibration I will show you miracles.* **"**

DAY 14

MORNING

1.
2.
3.

AFTERNOON

1.
2.
3.
4.
5.
6.

What is one aspect of your health that you're more grateful for?

Daily Affirmations

> ❖ **I have what it takes to reach my goals.** ❖

🌙 EVENING

> **❝ Fully inhale your dream and completely exhale manifestation of it. ❞**

DAY 15

MORNING

1.
2.
3.

AFTERNOON

1.
2.
3.
4.
5.
6.

What was something you did for the first time recently?

Daily Affirmations

- **I can handle anything that comes my way.**

EVENING

> To bring anything into your life, imagine that it's already there.

DAY 16

MORNING

1.
2.
3.

AFTERNOON

1.
2.
3.
4.
5.
6.

What are a few aspects of modern technology that you love?

Daily Affirmations

> **I always have enough money.**

🌙 EVENING

> **Manifest what you want into existence by opening up to the Universe. Let it be known!**

DAY 17

MORNING

1. _____
2. _____
3. _____

AFTERNOON

1. _____
2. _____
3. _____
4. _____
5. _____
6. _____

What is a small win that you accomplished in the past 24 hours?

— — — — — — — — — — — — — —   — — — — — — — — — —

Daily Affirmations

> ◆ **Everything I'm looking for I can find within me.** ◆

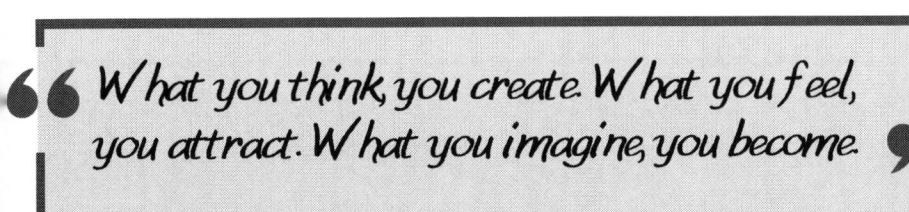

EVENING

> 66 *What you think, you create. What you feel, you attract. What you imagine, you become.* 99

DAY 18

MORNING

1.
2.
3.

AFTERNOON

1.
2.
3.
4.
5.
6.

What is your favorite season and what do you like about it?

Daily Affirmations

> ❖ **I have faith in myself and in my abilities.** ❖

EVENING

> 66 *Destiny is not a matter of chance, it is a matter of choice.* 99

DAY 19

MORNING

1. _____
2. _____
3. _____

AFTERNOON

1. _____
2. _____
3. _____
4. _____
5. _____
6. _____

What activity do you enjoy most when alone?

Daily Affirmations

> ❂ **Today I face everything with great courage.** ❂

EVENING

> " *Think the thought until you believe it, and once you believe it, it is.* "

DAY 20

MORNING

1. _____
2. _____
3. _____

AFTERNOON

1. _____
2. _____
3. _____
4. _____
5. _____
6. _____

What's the best gift you've ever received?
------------------ ------------------

Daily Affirmations

> **I see abundance everywhere.**

EVENING

> *We become what we think about. Energy flows where attention goes.*

DAY 21

MORNING

1.
2.
3.

AFTERNOON

1.
2.
3.
4.
5.
6.

What is the biggest accomplishment in your professional life?

Daily Affirmations

> ❂ **I live in perfect alignment with my highest truth.** ❂

EVENING

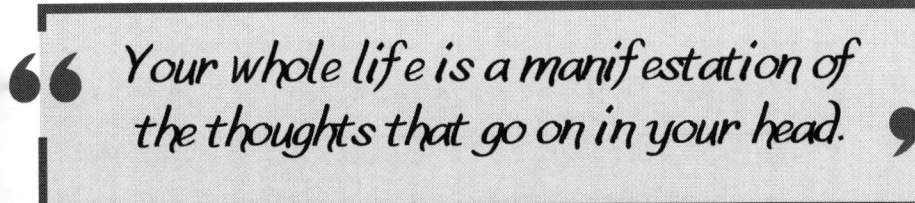

> " *Your whole life is a manifestation of the thoughts that go on in your head.* "

DAY 22

MORNING

1.
2.
3.

AFTERNOON

1.
2.
3.
4.
5.
6.

What are you most looking forward to this week?

Daily Affirmations

> **My intuition never lets me down.**

EVENING

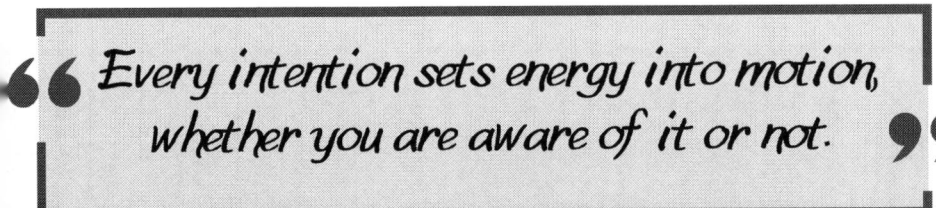

> *Every intention sets energy into motion, whether you are aware of it or not.*

DAY 23

MORNING

1.
2.
3.

AFTERNOON

1.
2.
3.
4.
5.
6.

What activity do you enjoy when with others?

Daily Affirmations

> ☾ I am focused, persistent and will never quit. ☽

EVENING

> " Whatever you create in your life you must first create in your imagination. "

DAY 24

MORNING

1. _____
2. _____
3. _____

AFTERNOON

1. _____
2. _____
3. _____
4. _____
5. _____
6. _____

What is your favorite emotion to feel?

Daily Affirmations

> **I am grateful for what I already have and for all that I receive now.**

EVENING

> *Once you make a decision, the universe conspires to make it happen.*

DAY 25

MORNING

1. _____
2. _____
3. _____

AFTERNOON

1. _____
2. _____
3. _____
4. _____
5. _____
6. _____

Name 3 things that always put a smile on your face

- -

Daily Affirmations

> **I am totally in charge of my life.**

EVENING

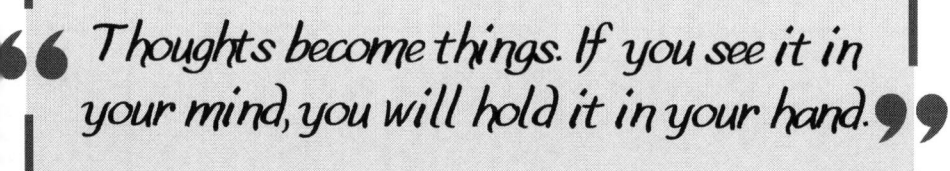

> *Thoughts become things. If you see it in your mind, you will hold it in your hand.*

DAY 26

MORNING

1.
2.
3.

AFTERNOON

1.
2.
3.
4.
5.
6.

What is something beautiful you saw today?

Daily Affirmations

> **I am fully supported making money doing what I love.**

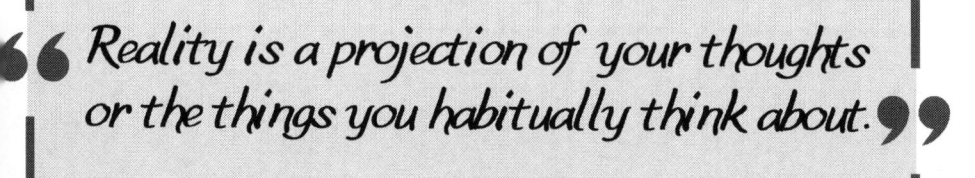

EVENING

> **Reality is a projection of your thoughts or the things you habitually think about.**

DAY 27

MORNING

1.
2.
3.

AFTERNOON

1.
2.
3.
4.
5.
6.

What meals do you most enjoy making or eating?

Daily Affirmations

I am in the process of becoming the best version of myself.

EVENING

> *Envision the future you desire. Create the life of your dreams. See it, feel it, believe it.*

DAY 28

MORNING

1.
2.
3.

AFTERNOON

1.
2.
3.
4.
5.
6.

What is your favorite time of day and why do you love it

Daily Affirmations

I am dedicated to living in alignment with my purpose.

EVENING

> *Go confidently in the direction of your dreams. Live the life you have imagined.*

DAY 29

MORNING

1.
2.
3.

AFTERNOON

1.
2.
3.
4.
5.
6.

Name one luxury you enjoy on a daily or weekly basis

Daily Affirmations

I am connected to the endless abundance of the universe.

EVENING

> **We receive exactly what we see. See yourself living in abundance and you will attract it.**

DAY 30

MORNING

1.
2.
3.

AFTERNOON

1.
2.
3.
4.
5.
6.

What is your favorite place in your home? Why?

Daily Affirmations

> **I have the courage to walk my own path and follow my dreams.**

EVENING

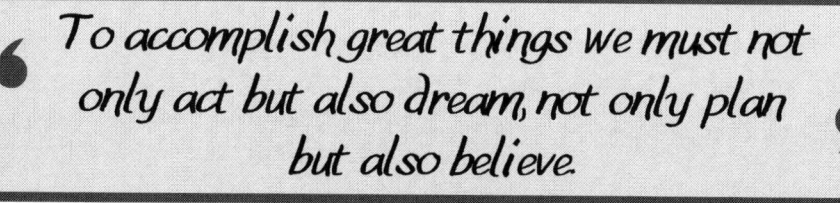

> *To accomplish great things we must not only act but also dream, not only plan but also believe.*

DAY 31

MORNING

1. _____
2. _____
3. _____

AFTERNOON

1. _____
2. _____
3. _____
4. _____
5. _____
6. _____

Who would you be if you could be someone else?

Daily Affirmations

> ❖ *I believe in myself and my ability to succeed.* ❖

EVENING

> " *Everyone visualizes whether he knows it or not. Visualizing is the great secret of success.* "

DAY 32

MORNING

1. _____
2. _____
3. _____

AFTERNOON

1. _____
2. _____
3. _____
4. _____
5. _____
6. _____

If you had unlimited money, what type of house would you buy
- -

Daily Affirmations

It is safe for me to make money.

EVENING

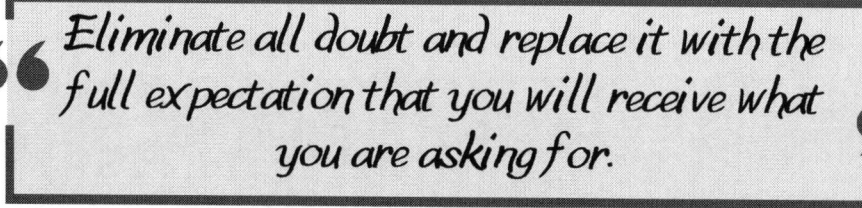

> *Eliminate all doubt and replace it with the full expectation that you will receive what you are asking for.*

DAY 33

MORNING

1.
2.
3.

AFTERNOON

1.
2.
3.
4.
5.
6.

If you could live anywhere, where would you live?

Daily Affirmations

> **I have the courage to keep going.**

EVENING

> "I attract into my life whatever I give my attention, energy, and focus to, whether positive or negative."

DAY 34

MORNING

1. _____
2. _____
3. _____

AFTERNOON

1. _____
2. _____
3. _____
4. _____
5. _____
6. _____

Who in your life is most important to you?

_ _

Daily Affirmations

> ◆ **Everything is alway working out for me.** ◆

🌙 EVENING

_____
_____
_____
_____
_____
_____
_____
_____
_____
_____
_____
_____
_____
_____
_____
_____
_____
_____
_____
_____
_____
_____

> ❝ *It is the combination of thought and love which forms the irresistible force of the law of attraction.* ❞

DAY 35

MORNING

1.
2.
3.

AFTERNOON

1.
2.
3.
4.
5.
6.

How would you feel if your desire manifested?

Daily Affirmations

> **My faith lifts me higher than fears.**

EVENING

> " *Whatever you can do, or dream you can, begin it. Boldness has genius, power, and magic in it. Begin it now.* "

DAY 36

MORNING

1.
2.
3.

AFTERNOON

1.
2.
3.
4.
5.
6.

Who made you smile in the past 24 hours and why?

Daily Affirmations

> **Everything feels so right;**
> **I trust I am on the right path for me.**

EVENING

> **" The true measure of success is how many times you can bounce back from failure. "**

DAY 37

MORNING

1.
2.
3.

AFTERNOON

1.
2.
3.
4.
5.
6.

What's something you have manifested recently?

Daily Affirmations

I handle success with grace.

EVENING

> *Reality is a projection of your thoughts or the things you habitually think about.*

DAY 38

MORNING

1.
2.
3.

AFTERNOON

1.
2.
3.
4.
5.
6.

How does it feel to be guided by the Universe?

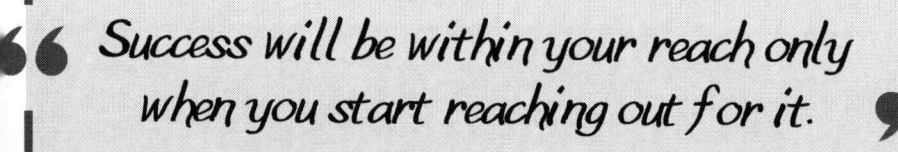

Daily Affirmations

> **My mind is free of resistance and open to the possibilities.**

EVENING

> *Success will be within your reach only when you start reaching out for it.*

DAY 39

MORNING

1.
2.
3.

AFTERNOON

1.
2.
3.
4.
5.
6.

What's the most recent miracle you've experienced?

Daily Affirmations

> **I am open to money coming to me from new ways that I've never imagined.**

EVENING

> **Your whole life is a manifestation of the thoughts that go on in your head.**

DAY 40

MORNING

1.
2.
3.

AFTERNOON

1.
2.
3.
4.
5.
6.

How can you cultivate more love in your life?

Daily Affirmations

> **I am creating the life I love.**

EVENING

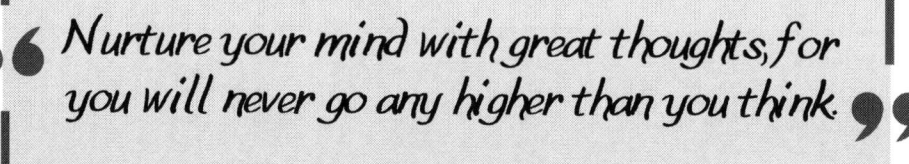

> " *Nurture your mind with great thoughts, for you will never go any higher than you think.* "

DAY 41

MORNING

1.
2.
3.

AFTERNOON

1.
2.
3.
4.
5.
6.

What is your intention for today?

Daily Affirmations

> **I trust myself and turn inward to seek my highest truth.**

EVENING

> " *What you radiate outward in your thoughts, feelings, mental pictures and words, you attract into your life.* "

DAY 42

MORNING

1.
2.
3.

AFTERNOON

1.
2.
3.
4.
5.
6.

What does your manifestation practice mean to you

Daily Affirmations

> **I am always being guided to living my heart's desires.**

EVENING

> ❝ That which you think, in any moment, attracts unto itself other thoughts that are like it. ❞

DAY 43

MORNING

1. _____
2. _____
3. _____

AFTERNOON

1. _____
2. _____
3. _____
4. _____
5. _____
6. _____

What are some things you want to do more of in your life

Daily Affirmations

> **My energy creates my reality.
> What I focus on is what I will manifest.**

🌙 EVENING

> *"You are a living magnet. What you attract into your life is in harmony with your dominant thoughts."*

DAY 44

MORNING

1.
2.
3.

AFTERNOON

1.
2.
3.
4.
5.
6.

List 3 things you can do to quickly shift your energy

Daily Affirmations

**I love the life I am creating
and opportunities flow to me with ease.**

EVENING

> *Whatever you hold in your mind on a consistent basis is exactly what you will experience in your life.*

DAY 45

MORNING

1.
2.
3.

AFTERNOON

1.
2.
3.
4.
5.
6.

How have you changed in the past months?

Daily Affirmations

> **My life works beautifully as I navigate my path with grace and ease.**

EVENING

> **Go confidently in the direction of your dreams. Live the life you have imagined.**

Inspiration Board:

Inspiration Board:

People I am grateful for:

1. _____
2. _____
3. _____
4. _____
5. _____

Things that make me happy:

1. _____
2. _____
3. _____
4. _____
5. _____

MY REFLECTIONS

MY REFLECTIONS

MY REFLECTIONS

MY REFLECTIONS

MY REFLECTIONS

SCAN ME

Discover More Products from Belffy Books

www.belffy.com

Printed by Amazon Italia Logistica S.r.l.
Torrazza Piemonte (TO), Italy